<u>Dedicated To:</u>
Father Luke Doyle

<u>Written By:</u> Abigail Gartland

Hello, my name is St. Luke!

I was born in Turkey in the very first century.

Hello, my name is St. Luke!

I was born in Turkey in the very first century.

I was a doctor and I spread the Word of God. I helped to heal bodies and souls.

I was honored to write and share the words of Jesus.

I was one of the four gospel writers. Mine is known as the most beautifully written.

The gospel is the written account of events that happened in Jesus' life.

While I was spreading the word of God, I followed St. Paul and took care of him when he was sick.

I stayed with St. Paul until he died.

Take a look at my gospel. You will see that it was written through the eyes of the Virgin Mother, Mary.

It was very important to me to share beautiful details about our Mother, Mary. My gospel is where the words for the "Hail Mary" prayer come from.

The Angel Gabriel greeted Mary by saying, "Hail Mary, favored one! The Lord is with you."

God's will for me was to write the stories of Jesus while he was on Earth.

Do you want to be more like me?

You can celebrate my feast day with me on October 18th

I pray for you every day of your life.

St. Luke, Pray for Us

pyright:

art: © PentoolPixie © LimeandKiwiDesigns
nsed purchased: 1/10/2024

About the Author

Abigail Gartland

I love the saints and I love my faith. The idea for sharing the stories of the saints with little ones came when my dear friend were expecting their first baby. I wanted t create something as unique and special as our friendship. Each book is dedicated to very special people and groups who have enriched my faith in different ways. I am blessed to write these stories and appreciate the unending support of my family and friends. When I am not writing am a middle school teacher. I hope you enjoy these stories. I pray for each and every person who opens one of my books to learn more about the saints.

Abbie